D1262223

Light from Dark Tombs

**A Traveler's Map to
Mysteries of
the Ancient Maya**

Mary Belle "Peg" Campbell

June 1991

Also by Mary Belle Campbell

A North Carolina Celebration
Moore County, USA

The Business of Being Alive,
Selected Poems

On the Summit—Bed and Breakfast
in the Swiss Alps—A Jungian Retreat

Light from Dark Tombs

**A Traveler's Map to
Mysteries of
the Ancient Maya**

*by
Mary Belle Campbell*

PERSEPHONE PRESS

Persephone Press Poetry Series No. 5

Thanks is given to archeologist and heart surgeon Dr. Francis Robicsek
of Charlotte, N.C., who graciously verified the bearded "Chinese" carving
at Copan, Honduras, as Stele "C," and to Harcourt Brace Jovanovich,
Inc. for use of brief quotes from T. S. Eliot's *Four Quartets*. Some of
these Mayan month timepoems have appeared in St. Andrews Review
and in Penelope Press Broadsides.

Library of Congress Cataloging in Publication Data

Campbell, Mary Belle Wertz, 1910 –

Light from Dark Tombs
— A Traveler's Map to Mysteries of the Ancient Maya

I. Title   1. Anthropology   2. Maya

90-060517

ISBN 0-9624737-9-0

Published by PERSEPHONE PRESS
Whispering Pines, NC 28327-9388

Adjunct to St. Andrews Press
St. Andrews College
Laurinburg, NC 28352

To My Traveling Companions — Here and Away

Contents

Preface

The Multiple Rhythms of Time

To the ancient Maya, time was no abstraction. It was inexorably alive, a divine entity existing without limits in either the past or the future, and Mayan culture was possessed by a passionate desire to measure and record its cyclic reality. Whichever Mayan dialect one studies, *kinh,* the glyph for sun/day/time, appears without fail in the various blossomings of its four-petaled flower. This long-ago vision of the mystery of time has now been given poetic expression by Mary Belle Campbell in her new collection of poems, a vision expressed nowhere so clearly as when she stands at twilight before Palenque's scrolled facade and sees

> the double helix of endless cycles,
> growth and drought,
> the fret of life and death —
> the renewal, after the fire.
> (Month 8 — UO: The *Paseo* Parade — Palenque)

These lines establish the psychic and poetic center of *Light from Dark Tombs: A Traveler's Map to Mysteries of the Ancient Maya.* Placing herself unashamedly in the tradition of the Mayan "daykeepers," the diviners who knew how to interpret the multiple rhythms of time, Mary Belle Campbell strives to bring what is dark into what Dennis Tedlock, in the introduction to his translation of the *Popul Vu,* calls "white clarity," that state of illumination toward which the world moves in the sacred Mayan text.

Mary Belle Campbell's fascination with ancient Mayan culture is an appropriate one, for what poet is not fascinated by time? From the metrical foundation of poetic craft to the ceaseless awareness of time passing, the way it doubles back, trips us, wears us down into dust, the poet is obsessed with the productions of time. For years, this particular poet has been obsessed with the creations of Mayan time. To discover for herself what remains of Mayan culture, she has traveled into Guatemala, Honduras, El Salvador, Yucatan, Quintana Roo and southern Mexico, often before there were adequate roads into the sites, circumventing the archeologists' donkey paths by flying with bush pilots in little three-place planes capable of landing in dry and fallow cornfields.

From both experience and imagination, she has created her own inter-connecting cycles in the voice of the Poet herself, the daykeeper who ultimately weaves all the voices together—the wisdom of her Maya archeologist-guide and the personalities of her two friends—one born into a British Columbia logging camp and the other a San Francisco probation officer disenchanted with North American materialism and failed criminology—her two traveling companions, who never met each other but with each of whom she planned these trips into well-researched archeological zones in alternate years, back in the 60's. Ultimately, the voice that comes through is an interweaving of all the voices of these places of power, making of each *stele*, each whisper of stone, breath of *copal* and sheaf of maize, its *ubixic*, its own unique "saying."

—Kathryn Stripling Byer, April 1990

Author of *The Girl in the Midst of the Harvest*, AWP Poetry Award Series Selection 1986, Texas Tech Press, Lubbock, Texas

Light from Dark Tombs

A Traveler's Map to
Mysteries of
the Ancient Maya

Antonio Mediz Bolio,
in a letter to Alfonso Reyes:

There is, in all these traditions, a very special kind of poetry, indigenous, mysterious, which springs from the remotest sources . . . . At times, in its expression and in its images, there may be found a certain similarity to the Oriental. This is precisely because all remnants of prehistoric America are marked with the same type of aesthetic and religious feeling that we associate with the Orient. Who can say that it is not rather the Orient that resembles America and that its roots were not on this continent? In any case, the character of the Maya is of this type and thus I have left it.

The Land of the Pheasant and the Deer: Folk Song of the Maya, 1935, Ediciones Dante, S.A., Calle 59 No.472, Merida, Yucátan, México

The multiplicity of the gods correspondeth
to the multiplicity of man.
　　　　　　　　— *C. G. Jung*

Prologue

Sightings — A Path Deep in the Jungle

And what the dead had no speech for, when living,
They can tell you, being dead: the communication
Of the dead is tongued with fire beyond the language of the living.
                    — T.S. Eliot, "Little Gidding," *Four Quartets*

First immigrants — long forgotten peaceable folk,
astronomer-priests, stone cutters and sculptors,
builders of temples and pyramid tombs —
their time-abraded, carved stones whisper their tales.

Tales of the Maya, written on turquoise water,
stored in bone marrow,
recalled from sun-kissed skin,
the trade winds' caresses,
surface in body memory of surging currents
plowed in longboats, shore-wise,
by island leaps, across a pacific sea.

Sighting an almost familiar coast,
they came ashore at the narrow waistline
of this giant continent,
America, before it was America —
tropical forests with towering fruit trees,
lowland swamps, lagoons of crystal water,
jungles bountiful as lands they left behind —
Asian lands, African, Man a migrant
from the beginning of humankind.

Did Mayan man wander north
from Zimbabwe's high plateau? Bury his bones
deep in Olduvai Gorge? Was it they
who paused to build the pyramids of Gizeh?
tombs in the Valley of the Kings?

What dreams prompted a poet
to pause in his wanderings, to chisel a line
in three alphabets on the Rosetta Stone?
One line of hieroglyphics in three alphabets . . . .

What early engineers, serious
as children building sandcastles and moats,
designed truncated pyramids as lofty platforms
for temples, structured aqueducts and canals
to channel the waters that made
the Tigris and Euphrates Valley bloom?

The Maya — with sun-bronzed Asian faces,
tall foreheads board-flattened at birth —
did they fashion the flowering temples
of Babylon? carve the Persian stones
at Persepolis long buried? design
the ziggurat of Ur, these towering monuments
to human pride, human spirit?
Who is to say?

Legend recounts they came in longboats
directly from the west, the ancient east.
In what forests of China, Malaysia
did they fell great cedars to chisel
their dug-out, out-rigger canoes?
Faces of today's Mayas — the only clues.

In time's round, island hopping,
they came ashore,
climbed the spine of their new island,
heard volcanoes grumble like island gods
welcoming them home.

While Europe's and Asia's Huns,
horse-riding Mongols, Goths,
sea-faring Vikings, Angles and Saxons
raped, plundered, burned,
and Christian knights
massacred in the name of God,
Mayas knew. Knew secret things.

Knew the Way,
the way of the heart, the way of the stars.
The way, some say, to—the stars.

December-January-February-March
—MAC-KANKIN-MUAN-PAX-KAYAB

The Music of the Mayan Calendar—1961

Ancient Maya had ears for the Eternal Song.
Migrating, crossing the far-flung Mayab,
they transported their Ancient Wisdom,
holy as the Tabernacle to Moses,
and like Assyrian astrologers,
charted the sun as it cycles the heavens
in years of eighteen months,
months of twenty-days,
plus five New Year days—the Mayan
calendar more accurate than Julius Caesar's
or Pope Gregory's—the one we use today.

Astronomers, mathematicians
of ingenious invention, they visualized
time cycles as interlocking wheels,
saw the centuries turn the millennia,
function like the works of a giant pocketwatch.
Mayas knew exactly . . . How many millennia ago?

At Chichén Itzá in Yucatán,
Mayan scientist-priests, sky gazing
from the ramp-ascending observatory,
the snail *el Caracol*,
counted All Time sacred, pictured
each of the twenty days of the month
with a different glyphic face,
each day, a god of serious mien.
They named the eighteen months

with handsome, power-filled heads
of monsters they could respect — symbols
that spoke to them of gods and goddesses
dispensing favors — yellow sunlight,
drizzling rain, plentiful game, blossoms,
and the pollinating work of bees.

Totem faces and esoteric designs
mask their hieroglyphic calendar,
mark the seasons in Codices — fan-folded books
of paper pounded of fig bark or henequen —
record dates of rituals and feast days
to celebrate seeding and harvest
in dance and song.

Mayan books read like almanacs:
prescriptions for clouds — bountiful Dragons,
and thunder — Celestial Serpents,
all Nature, beneficent deities,
though Terror, Truce, and Joy
comprise the scale of their gifts.
The Maya, at One with Trinity,
Earth, Sun and Rain,
aware of Eternal Song, Centerpoint,
fulcrum, fragile balance
in Nature and Mankind.

Month 1 — MAC — December

The Dry Season — Chichén Itzá, Yucatán, México — 1961, 1986, 1987

Winter, in Yucatán,
in a region never winter,
savors the dry season
on the calendar's thirsting tongue,
mouths the names of five twenty-day
months — MAC, KANKIN, MUAN, PAX, KAYAB —
months dry, gutteral, rasping
as squawks of jungle maccaws.

EB-day, dark day of winter solstice —
its glyph, a sad little face
with turned-down mouth,
an omen-filled day — shun death and water!

Autumn's clock-like turning
slows, grinds,
halts for three days, overcast,
Earth out of tune, men estranged.
Both Earth and man know drought,
when seed and spirit, in parching wind,
harden outer shells.

Dry season — periodic sleep for seeds,
siesta for mankind —
when resources stored in darkness

ripen, ache to burst,
suffer to be born, and to grow—
Man only dimly conscious, unlike
the nut-like mahogany seed
aware of its destiny.

When rituals, chanted
and danced to exhaustion,
produce only sun and overcast,
man and seed sleep.

> *Each in his cycle,*
> *rouses from underground,*
> *extends hands, roots, fingers*
> *like tendril coils,*
> *knows the dark music*
> *in the germinating kernel,*
> *energized to reach*
> *for returning Light.*

Month 2 — KANKIN — December-January

Answer to the Dry Season — Chac Mool the Rain God

In this season of shortest days
when light rains crystal as spirit,
and Yucatán's cloudless skies fail
to nourish the thin body
of the Earth Mother,
hope, ripe with seed, shrivels
in the clatter of gourd-dry
frangi-pani trees —
hope tainted with the smell
of summer drought,
like meat tinged with suspicion.
In desperation, priest and chieftain,
forced to act, respond.

They stand before the temple
on top of *el Castillo*,
many-tiered pyramid at Chichén Itzá,
towering above the ceremonial plaza
in geometric splendor, as at Gizeh,
like Gizeh, sepulcher to One,
and to thousands who fell to raise it up.

The Chief of Itzas —
in plumed ceremonial headdress
of red, green and blue feathers

from the sacred Quetzal bird —
stands with the High Priest,
the two most kingly,
mesmerized —
by pride and by fear —
to perform the sacrifice.

A young boy,
the Chieftain's youngest son
lies stretched out on his back
on the low stone Jaguar altar —
like a young Jaguar about to be skinned,
held down by arms and legs
by four kneeling slaves, naked
but for a string about the waist.

The Priest swings
the ceremonial stone axe.
One shriek
plummets down to the plaza
thronging with artisans and slaves.
One cry
pierces the ears
of the roiling populace below,
one cry
of a rich tomorrow sacrificed,
cut down, harvested like corn,
to feed the multitude.

The flint-sharpened stone blade
broaches the ribcage.
Blood sprays to slake the thirst
of Rain God Chac Mool.

With obsidian knife
the Priest carves, lifts out
the pulsing heart — sanctified.

Knotted cords rise
on the neck of the boy's father.
Cumulous thunderheads
billow and tower on horizon.

His tears and the god's tears,
fall on parched fields,
the limestone breast of Chi-chén It-zá.

Month 3 — MUAN — January-February

Mayan Books — The Codices
Ordered Destroyed — 1527 A.D.

Within twenty years
of Columbus' sighting the Yucatán shore,
Spanish *Conquistadores*
invaded the Mayab on horseback.
Hordes of conquering soldiers
in metal helmets and breastplates,
followed by priests and masons,
swept over the Land of the Maya.

Spanish Bishop Diego Landa,
as exhuberant in his passion
to Christianize the Indians
as in his zeal to design
baroque facades for his churches,
suspected the Mayas' fan-folded books
might be their Bibles.
He ordered adobe huts ransacked,
Mayan books seized and burned
in great bonfires illuminating
the graceful, benevolent rooflines
of village churches,
a fire still burning.

Like the Egyptians and the Chinese,
the Maya invented paper

in prehistoric ages
by pounding soaked fibers —
fig bark, palmetto or henequin — into mash,
rolled thin into long sheets,
folded when dry into folios of
pleated pages, flaring and wide
as a *señorita's* skirt.

Far from religious laws, Mayan Codices
were books of early science,
charts of circling sun and planets,
like almanacs, guides for plantings,
feast days and rituals.

Few of these ancient Codices exist.
Three were found on dusty shelves
in Madrid, Paris and Dresden libraries
dating back to the Spanish Conquest,
gifts to European Kings.

Mayan scribes and artists painted
their language on paper and plaster, carved
their symbols on stone, clay and stucco —
beautiful glyphs, stylized faces:
man, bird, animal, monster
to stand for days, months, years
and longer cycles of Time.
Glyphs of squared circles,
represented the stuff of their lives —
woven reed mats, ears of corn,
leaves of corn, corn tassels,
theirs, a maize culture,
corn the staple and the art.

With bars and dots, they counted —
a dot for one, a bar for five,

with a shell-like little face for twenty,
the sign for completion, as on the last day
of their twenty-day month.

One, any one of these ancient lost Codices
might have contained a clue
to a full translation of the inscriptions
on pyramids, temples, *stelae* and tombs,
just possibly—a New World Rosetta Stone.

Month 4 — PAX — February

Moon Goddess X-chel and God Jaguar

Into this dry season of short days
and long nights, comes PAX,
month of Luna, Night Sun,
linked to God Jaguar
in Underworld Heaven.

That dark phantom, animal hunger,
sacred need for periodic closeness,
crawls in the veins,
pounces without warning
in tender embraces, or seduces
with the Horned Serpent's
wily promises,
as the Chinese ancients knew.

In the depths of night,
God Jaguar roams village paths,
paces walls of ceremonial centers,
encounters one and all,
descends at daybreak
to coil with the Serpent God
in *Metnal*, Underworld Heaven,
the cave where the Sun goes at night,
a place of shining Light.

From this union, springs MANIK,

name day of Black Hunter,
Scorpion god of black merchants,
immigrants from the east,
who sailed, paddled, poled
up-river as far as La Venta —
where black men carved and polished
monuments to their heritage —
gigantic, thirty-ton negroid heads
six feet in diameter,
rafted out of the jungle,
memorials to their early arrival,
their god, progeny of Night Sun Luna
and Rain God Chac.

By night Luna pulls on the tides
and on the tides in arteries
of animal and man,
as Sun by day draws almost visible rays
from rain-sated earth and argent sea.
By night black-spotted Jaguar wakens,
prowls village paths, sneaks
under hammocks in bamboo huts,
yellow cat eyes flashing in moonlight.

Luna — Moon Goddess X-chel — glides
across the translucent globe of sky.
Chac, her old and temperamental lover,
now gentle, now wild, wakens,
inhales a sharp rush of air,
flashes eyes, grumbles,
in a rumble . . . of thunder . . . .

Dark cumulous billows tower, scud
across Luna's gold mask,
golden as Agamemnon's.
Careless,

Chac vents his unconcern, careless
as mortal man.
A downpour douses the fields,
slakes the parched throat of Earth.
Goddess X-chel appears for a moment,
lemon-yellow in the haze,
sinks down, drops below horizon.
The dry season ends . . . .

When Earth and Moon conjoin
and Jaguar stalks the white night,
spring rains commence.
The Lunar New Year magnetizes,
cracks open the shells of dormant seeds.
Maize, squash, beans, melons sprout,
nourished by water more precious
than jade.

Bursting tendrils
nurse at the breast of Earth,
night of the moon goddess X-chel . . . .
X-chel, Angel and Dragon,
guards her sister planet Earth.
Wise, knowing her own fate,
she watches over Earth's birth, flowering
and death . . . .

> *The Earth Mother three times effaced —*
> *by Flood,*
> *by Quake,*
> *by Winds — Winds of Hurricane Force.*
> *Three worlds, three times destroyed.*
> *Three times, remade.*
> *This, the Fourth World.*

Mayan skywatchers augur an end.

They reach to understand the prophecy,
to foresee — and to warn.
They follow X-Chel's swift
and graceful turning,
her eighteen twenty-day pirouettes.

Three times they chart
the choreography
of Earth's dance through fixed stars,
and like the Babylonians,
they re-compile the Ephemeris,
search with growing awareness —
for a God who will restore
the faith of man in his own seed,
as he trusts
in the seeds of the harvest —
for an Order that will tell them
by what name
to call a God who will answer
their innermost cry —
a God rooted within,
thirsting to be called.

Month 5 — KAYAB — February-March

Slash and Burn — Ritual of Fire

The old gods do not die.
In Yucatán, in Dry Season,
needle-like leaves of felled pines
rust red as clay
against the fawn-colored straw
of last year's vegetation, red
as tongues of flame licking
Yucatán's thin limestone earth.

Smoke from cleared fields —
like resinous smoke of burning *copal*
from Chichicastenango altars —
wafts Mayan prayers skyward
to Rain God Chac — the ritual,
slash and burn, slash and burn.

Flame reverberates — like thunder,
licks up the rusty branches,
petitions, begs rain.
Denuded fields cry their dry tears,
dust in the wind,
the burning branches, a green sacrifice
of twenty years' growing
turned to white ash
to fertilize the stony ground . . .
for how many centuries?
and how many yet to come?

Part II   Introduction to Vernal Equinox

March, April, May—KUMKU, POP, UO, ZIP, ZOTZ

The Tree of Life Embracing Death

Come spring—breeze-sweet season
of equinoctial crossing—
when Sun, soaring Earth's ecliptic
northward, pauses to rest for a day,
like migrating sea birds—wandering albatross,
pelicans swooping down in ragged V's
to sandbars off-shore.

Vegetation, dormant as man's faith,
rallies at first peep of tree frogs.
Mahogany seeds sprout from burst shells,
confirm myths of destiny, as stars do,
those archipelagos of islands
in the sea of sky.

Spendthrift nature spills her seed
on the bone-rich breast of Yucatán.
Fruit ripens as buds open.
Wild orchids flourish in trees,
Chiapas and Tabasco teem
with damp and mildew,
Nature progressing to Death, and Rebirth.

Come spring, we are all one body—
we are Earth, part of the Great Round
of Earth Mother responding to Chac Mool.

> *Like vines we climb*
> *a Tree of Life,*

our arms reaching out
like branches into Space
beyond the tomb,
as on the lid
of the sarcophagus
at Palenque.

Born blind, we climb
inside a Pyramid
of four dimensions,
the climb within,
from wellspring to tomb,
the deepest, steepest climb.

As at Gizeh, so at Chichén Itzá,
Uxmal, Palenque, Cobá, Tikal,
we strive for pinnacles,
find fallen stones,
each a building stone.

Month 6 — KUMKU — April

The Remote Lacandóne Indians — Chiapas Jungle, México — 1963

A mantle of humidity cloaks
the wide lowland valley of the vast,
fast-flowing Usmacinta River,
as it courses, swollen, along the border
of Chiapas, México's steamiest state.
Vines hang like ropes from tall trees
reaching for sunlight — a dark canopy
above the entangled rain forest,
la Selva Lacandona.

Here, long-haired Lacandónes,
more remote than Amazonian Indians,
live unspoiled —
except for matches, combs and candy
dropped off by a bush pilot
flying the occasional adventurer to Bonampak,
the German woman anthropologist to Yaxchilán.

Far from road and railroad,
inaccessible except by jungle trek
with donkey and *machete,* or downstream
from Sayaxche by dugout canoe,
or by bush pilot in three-place Cessna 180,
these true Mayas hold to the vision
of their rich prehistory,

their three- to ten- to twenty-thousand-year
civilization—the best estimates, hazy.

Unique among Maya living today
in the rain forest Mayab—range of Mayas—
the Lacandóne keep their ancient dynamism alive
through archaic rituals.
They meditate,
breathe resinous smoke
as it rises from clay bowls,
veiled in clouds of Unknowing,
an energy beyond understanding.
They dress in loosely woven, ankle-length,
white cotton ponchos,
speak their own Lacandón language.

>   *But for how long before oil rigs,*
>   *company stores, truck trails*
>   *surround their reserve?*
>   *and refugees fleeing Guatemala's*
>   *civil warfare transmit their plagues*
>   *to the untamed jungle?*

The Lacandóne, the one true stock of Maya,
hold to the old ways,
as the woven reed mat—a throne—passes
from the last Chieftain—Eagle Man—
to his daughter—Eagle Woman.
She trains her son, already a young man,
to take her place one day.
Poems lurk in his eyes.

As Chief, she defends the past
against the future,
her power threatened with erosion—
by crosswinds more potent

than the nun's schoolroom down river,
the yellow plastic bucket
reaching into her airy
thatched bamboo shelter
with its crude table, two benches,
two hammocks.

The material world menaces
Earth Mother's children —
all organisms rooted in Earth's crust.
Looters invade the Lacandón Biosphere —
threaten the Eternal Now
remembered in the ways of Old Chief,
by his daughter, his grandson,
lighting with a burning stick
from their campfire
little pots of incense
for their meditative silences.

Each year before the dry season ends,
Lacandón men and women priests —
each worker, a priest educated in Mayan lore —
the entire tribe gathers, swarms
like worker ants over the jungle loam.
They drill with planting sticks,
bury kernels of maize —
corn developed by their ancestors
from primitive grasses —
and seeds of beans, squash and cotton
in cleared fields, deep hidden
in *la Selva Lacandona.*

UAYEB — Five Ominous New Year Days — APRIL

The New Solar Year — Copán, Honduras — 1965

Governments report the archeological centers closed: Quiriguá in Guatemala due to bandits on the road; Copán in Honduras, for unrest at the border. Airlines send flights off early when disorderly crowds gather. The American Consul advises arriving businessmen and lady archeologists to take the next flight out when a general strike in San Salvador blocks the streets, closes the hotel. But the gods still inhabit the ceremonial sites, and they speak, though there are few who will listen.

Fearful, transcendent Presence,
unspeakable Great Mother-Father God,
the Sun . . . the unknown power within . . .
the New Solar Year.

New Years — an Asian Holy Week remembered
in crossing the Arctic Land Bridge —
if indeed they came that way —
or retained like the polar star
in migrations east by water.

UAYEB, ambiguous as
its two-faced Vulture glyph,
door to a new beginning
like the three-day Chinese New Year.
Five equinoctial days
precede the Solar Year
beginning at the Vernal Equinox —
days for contemplation,

fasting, prayers for the dead.

Not dead, but alive
on a non-material plane
of faster energy cycles,
invisible, though
sometimes a presence nudges.
We speak, ask for insight . . .
for Light into dark questions.

We want answers — to questions
too deep to put into words,
instant answers, solid,
smooth as great stones tumbled
down the rowdy Copan River
eroding the acropolis foundations,
answers like polished gem stones,
edges worn smooth
by generations of experience.

On the eve of UAYEB — five unlucky days —
paths through Copan village empty
at dusk. Only the Mayan merchant
remains in the *Cantina* —
lest *el Brujo*, the medicine man,
need an herbal, a tribal remedy
to soothe a hysterical patient,
the year's chosen guilt punishing the body
with itching welts, a sneezing attack.

Ever a Garden of Eden for ancient Maya,
the Copan Valley blooms at all seasons,
produces tobacco, maize, continuous
crops of beans, melons, squash,
shows no evidence of warfare,
drought or famine.
No explanation for the disappearance
of a flourishing society

at the height of its artistic achievements . . .
only those death's head sculptures
beyond the ceremonial zone hint of change.

> *Are we all one people*
> *dispersing in two directions,*
> *circling the globe —*
> *to the East and to the West —*
> *forgetting one long-ago beginning?*

An instinctive dread
pervades the quiet at UAYEB,
the atmosphere heavy with rancid smoke
floating in at sundown — an archaic rite
retained in the migration of a culture,
animal sacrifice outside the village.

To reinforce ancestral views of the cosmos,
they practise an esoteric ceremony,
a communion table spread on the ground
with small pots of corn gruel for the gods
and copper bells to get their attention.

When the church bell sounds,
the *Indios* tremble, give thanks.
The priest erases the Old Year,
banishes Evil
from its scavenging Vulture face.

> *Mayas, they contain their terror,*
> *compose to the Wholeness within.*
> *Light shines from a New Solar Year.*
> *They acknowledge Good and Evil —*
> *Beauty and Horror — reconciled.*

Month 7 — POP — April

The Lacandóne Planting Festival
— Bonampak, Chiapas

Fields planted, the Lacandóne Maya
drop their planting sticks,
prepare for purification ceremonies —
UAYEB — the five-day Solar New Year —
awaits the Equinox . . . .

They remain inside their huts,
consecrate themselves
in arcane ceremonies for one more year
to the ways of their ancestors.

After five meditative, guilt-resolving days,
Chief Eagle Woman,
dons her father's handwoven mantle,
his rustling corn-tasseled headdress
and leads her band of flowing-haired Mayas
in a raucous, day-long, red-bannered
procession through the mahogany forest
to the after-planting festival at Bonampak.

They join their Maya cousins
before the ruined city's hillside temple,
where bright murals painted on plaster
show peasants and prisoners tortured,
executed by chiefs more autocratic

than ancient Maya priests
or today's gentle Lacandónes
following a simple life
in long-hidden jungle retreats —
rumors of head-hunting to the contrary.

At dusk, like luna moths drawn to firelight,
Mayan farmers gather to circle the bonfire
in front of the *Great Stele* —
broken, monumental stone portrait
of Great Chief, formidable in aspect,
accoutrement of feathers and jewels
designed to intimidate.

Seated in a circle on woven reed mats,
token seats of authority,
Lacandon chiefs recount tales
of earlier, gentler centuries
before insurgent workers
revolted against cruel punishment
at the hands of Mexican Toltecs
infiltrating from the north,
materialistic and drunk with power.
The murals painted here celebrate
their taking over Mayan laborers and slaves.

> *Vivid paintings in primary colors*
> *enliven plaster walls of niches built*
> *into the face of the Temple of Bonampak.*
> *War scenes — infighting*
> *with spears and arrows,*
> *blood-letting rites of torture,*
> *stingray spines jabbing*
> *prisoners' fingers,*
> *self-inflicted stabbings*
> *of the foreskin by priests*

intent on pleasing
Toltec Gods of War.

Acrid smoke from *ocote* pine boughs
fills the plaza. Fog drifts in.
Farmers jostle nearer the ceremonies.

From low auditory chambers high up
the face of the Temple, built to amplify
the sound, notes from double flutes of clay
drop down through layers of smoke,
music liquid as raindrops.

> *Cantors chant, incant,*
> *for the dry season to break.*
> *Priests intone*
> *for rain to swell the planted seeds.*
> *Shamans call for sacrifice.*

In solemn procession, the Maya place
food and flowers on eroded stone altars.
No more living sacrifices —
Lacandónes are twentieth century Maya.

Still, they preserve the ways of their fathers,
honor the souls of bush brothers,
totem animals, Bat and Cougar, Monkey and Dog.
They listen to whispers of *sapodilla*
and mahogany trees,
answer with meditation and dance.

> *They CHEW the DREAM-rich buds*
> *of pey-O-tl, and they DANCE*
> *to the OLD and the O-min-ous*
> *IN-can-TA-tion of the UN-*
> *stopped BEAT*

and the ONE-two, ONE-two
of the WEDGE-shaped
IX-ta-PAN-tl DRUM
and the DEEP-er VOICE
of the TREE-STUMP DRUM . . . .

Mayan chiefs, priests, shamans,
triangles of power, sit like Hindu Yogis,
meditate to embrace the Source,
to sustain the power to preserve their Myth —
their spirit — the MANA — within.
Midnight at Bonampak — shadows
fill the plaza below the Temple facade.
Drums slow, dance ends in trance.

They break their fast,
feast on fruit of mango and *sapote*,
on roast tapir and peccary,
yams, breadfruit, tomatoes, pimientos
sheathed in palm leaves,
baked all day in the arms of Earth.
They sip the sacred juice
of the maguey century plant
from bowls painted blue
to mark the New Solar Year,
bowls blue as priestly auras.

A light rain begins —
scarcely more than day's-end humidity,
but a sign — end of the Dry Season,
Man and Earth re-born.
They mouth the open sound of the Universe:

Ommmmmmmmmmmmm . . .
reverberating . . .
the magic O, Zero,

civilization's
tremendous discovery . . .
resounds — down the millions of days,
thousands of years —
in inventories of stored cotton and corn.
The magic O — Zero —
sings in Codices, in charts,
the five Planets moving through the seasons,
the click of interlocking wheels —
clocking off each day,
each year, of the Calendar.

The music of lost Codices echoes,
silent clay whistles,
back to the Beginning, to 3,114 B.C. —
more than a million days,
Mayan Sources hidden in clouds of Zeros,
in the flight of constellations
through the Zodiac . . . .
The circle Zero — a Serpent with its tail
in its mouth, sign of Completion —
End — and Beginning — One Whole —
Mankind's greatest wisdom.

Priests of Lacandóne tribes
know Wholeness, the Three-in-One,
relay such Light to sons and daughters.

Eagle Woman's son — "Crown Prince"
the *Anglos* call him —
flies out to market in Palenque
whenever bush pilots drop down into cornfields
and will promise to bring him back again.
Already he lives in two worlds,
as immature Western civilization
encroaches on his emerald forest.

When Eagle Woman, true to ideas
of Old Chief, dies,
her son may leave and not return,
and these remnants of ancient Maya,
like the Maya of ancient cities,
will disappear, each a temple surrendered,
lost to the jungle again.

MONTH 8 — UO — May

The *Paseo* Parade — Palenque Village, Chiapas, México — 1963

After the dry season burn-off of fields,
the boys' burn-off of childhood,
Mayan farmers — *campesinos* — rest
by day on their folded *serapes*
in the shade of breadfruit trees.
Waxy leaves like giant hands gently wave,
fan their bronze skin, lull them into dreams.
They doze in soft, tropical air.

Their women huddle over little fires
in smoke-raddled huts,
bake *tortillas* on tiles
for *la cena*, late evening supper,
babies tugging at long skirts.

At sundown, temperature drops,
breezes flow in, and whole families flock
to *el centro*, whirring like doves at twilight.

The *jugo combo* of drums, jugs and guitars
strikes up a haunted music invoking spirits.
The *paseo* begins, circles the plaza
between *la Iglesia Santa Maria* and *la Cantina*.
Women and girls, giggling, stroll
arm in arm, three abreast, clockwise;

boys and men circle widdershins —
in the opposite direction —
looking them over, exchanging signs,
making dates in passing.

Two *aficionadas de cosas mayas,*
would-be archeologists out of step with time,
stand at twilight before the façade
of Palenque's stucco church
with its baroque Mayan scrolls —

> *double helix of endless cycles,*
> *growth and drought,*
> *fret of life and death,*
> *renewal after the fire.*

Inside *Santa Maria,* smoking candles
flicker like fireflies in the haze of spring.
Señoras complete the Stations of the Cross,
kneel at one altar after another,
light candles
against the darkness of their lives.

Like their ancestors, the Maya
remember what most *Anglos* forget —
they live in Eternity — now.

They wait for a Fire Storm . . .
not with impatience.
They romp and they dance,
wait for spring, wait for an answer.
The flame of thorn and pine —
annual ritual
burn-off of field and forest
depleted of minerals —
burns brighter than a thousand candles —

Green Sacrifice to Trinity,
Sun, Earth and Rain.

At morning mass the Mayan
brother priest warns:

> *Your Guardian Angel waits*
> *on your awareness.*
>
> *Today's men in the towns*
> *spend their silver,*
> *dress like the Spanish,*
> *sell the gold chains*
> *from their wives' necks,*
> *ceaselessly running, gathering,*
> *devouring, whoring, warring.*
>
> *Endlessly, they will tramp*
> *the Calendar round,*
> *eyes averted*
> *from interlocking wheels*
> *of Mayan Time,*
> *blind to the brass ring*
> *forged and hammered*
> *by their ancestors,*
> *on which they could swing*
> *upward.*

Month 9 — ZIP — May-June

Dinner with *el Junglero* — Palenque Village — 1963

The tropical Sun drops crimson
and fast as Newton's apple.
Fingers of pink-gold
clutch at daylight, stir fading blue
to lavender evening.
The cooling dark
strokes bare shoulders.
A light stir of air moves in
from surrounding jungle.

In plastic boots we walk
the muddy village road,
wade the one block to the jungle edge,
to the one restaurant,
a board shack,
weather-beaten and without windows,
its plank door, like the Gate of Hades,
entrance to another world,
neither Mayan nor Western,
but an island in Time,
swept by opposing currents.

Eyes, out of joint,
focus slowly, adjust to a dim interior.
Two lanterns hang from nails

on rough-sawn mahogany walls.

The tawny, spotted skin of a Jaguar
and two black-on-white stone rubbings
transfigure the smoky atmosphere —
a panel of glyphs
from the Temple of the Sun
and a tracing
of an angular-faced Mayan chief
seated like a Hindu yogi
under a headdress of animal masks
and tassels of corn . . . .

At two tables pushed together,
a motley herd of ranchers
in high-heeled boots
and flat-brimmed Spanish cowboy hats
are laughing and shouting
over their drinks.
Presently, they drift off,
all but one stubby little man
with muscles like hawsers.

> *Buena noche,* I say,
> Wouldn't you like to join us?

> *Si, gracias.* I'm hungry.
> I thought those cattlemen
> would never get off their asses
> and into their Jeeps
> and head back to their ranches.

> Ooh, my head . . . . What's for supper?
> Veal stew?
> Fine, and a cup of coffee.

Lo siento, Señoras,
excuse me.
I forget what it's like —
dining with broads — I mean — ladies.

Me? Do?
I'm a *junglero* — a jungle man —
a surveyor.

Si, Norte Americano,
but I've lived all my life
on the edge,
between two lost civilizations —
the Mayan,
and the North American —
one gone for good,
and the other going fast,
and for some of the same reasons, too —
no sacred sense of self.

Yeah, I've been in the States
got my training there, but you can have it —
the crowds, the noise,
the crime on the streets,
the corruption, the costs,
the yippies, yuppies, druggies —
and suburbanites,
still after the lost American dream.

And civil rights, my Gawd,
how you can evaluate a man
or a woman by color . . . .
Down here we range from pink to brown,
to black, to purple.

Sure, there's class distinction —

but it's based on what a man can do —
and real discrimination against women,
except among the Maya —
but no discrimination, as to color.

Well, maybe some among pure Spanish,
but even their daughters
at the University are marrying
mestizo doctors and physicists.

But back home, the stress, the traffic,
the fears that strangle the songs
of immigrants crowding your cities,
of migrants harvesting your
fields and orchards.
The way you spoil your wilderness areas,
the countryside,
the city highway strips . . .
ears deaf to all but what a buck will buy.
A lot of it's happening in Mexico, too.

Here in the jungle, though,
it's beautiful — birdsong at dawn,
and so quiet at night
you can hear a howler monkey, or a cougar,
half a mile away.

All I need out here
is my *hamaca*, my *machete*,
my instruments — and a mule,
and I'm all set.

How about you two coming with me?
I'll be back in a week.
I can get two extra donkeys and two hammocks.

No? Too bad,
you'd have a lot more fun out where
I'm going, than here,
climbing over these ruined temples,
that pyramid. Personally,
I can't stand civilization!

Say, I've got me a lottery ticket.
Here, you take it,
and when you get back to Mexico,
if it's any good, it's all yours.

Sure enjoyed listening to you two.
Quite a change for me. *Buena noche!*

Buena suerte! Good luck to you!

June-July-August-September
— ZOTZ-TZEC-XUL-YAXKIN-MOL

Warning Signs

Planet Venus waking from her nether world
sleep with Winter, somersaults from West to East,
rises before dawn as Morning Star.
Solstice — a time to be wary,
its glyph LAMAT, a Mayan Satyr
with head of Dog, haunches of Jaguar,
a mischievous sower of discord.

At each marked stone notch
throughout the Mayab,
as at Stonehenge, heelstone to altarstone,
midsummer dawn glistens straight in —
as on the first day of Spring
when the Sun God transfixes his followers.

His first ray, like an arrow,
enters the slit in the stone
of Chichén Itzá's towering,
snail-designed *el Caracol* — a ramp-ascending,
limestone-white observatory.
Wordless, bird-like warbling
glides over the ceremonial plaza,
temple maidens, vaguely prescient of disaster.

Solstice, a day when the Sun God
reaches his northernmost stretch, pauses
to celebrate the year's longest day,
rests on the celestial equator

midpoint between spring
and autumn Equinoxes,

For three Jaguar nights
the far-off Celestial Music
swells to cacophony under the stars,
then silence,
Good on balance with Evil, Body with Soul,
as with the Chinese at New Year.

Light winds of evening
play like grace notes
over bronzed bodies dancing,
glorify summer, as Mercury, twin of Venus,
rises in the darkening west —
on the horn of the young Moon.

The Sun goes underground,
bonfires appear on the hills,
celebrate Midsummer Eve —
a night when spirits fly in the sparks,
dance in Midsummer haze,
a night for merrymaking, feasting and *pulque*.

Shoulders rotate
to the rhythm of seasons,
arms, wrists, fingers, legs, toes cavort,
workers caught in primitive mind,
one with Nature in the Corn Dance.

> *The hierarcy beguiled by power and possessions,*
> *ignores a day of unexplained darkness,*
> *a night of choking air,*
> *a sullenness among the workers,*
> *the corona around the Moon — a warning sign.*

Month 10 – ZOTZ – June

The Yucatán Cave Where the Sun Goes at Night – 1961

Mesoamerica – Middle America –
narrow waist
joining the upper and lower bodies
of the continent –
supports a fragile land of contrasts:
a backbone of volcanoes,
restless subterranean rumblings,
dense jungles, alluvial swamps.

Yucatán, a dry shelf of limestone,
tunneled with underground streams and caves
used for thousands of years,
not for shelter,
but by a hierarchy of priests
for their Sacred Mysteries.

A snout-nosed glyph names the month ZOTZ
for the Leaf-Nosed Bat,
one more mask of the One God,
many-faced, yet faceless, un-named,
a name never to be called.

Each night at twilight,
this shadowy, bat-shaped God
quits the shade of banana trees,

seeks water, sips in an ominous
swoop over the *Cenote,*
a broad, deep well, sacred sinkhole,
broad and deep as hope,
where the thin, limestone crust
of this peninsula —
tenuous as life itself —
has collapsed to sweet underground water.
Steep-walled *Cenote,* gluttonous maw,
where workers, artisans, priests,
even Maya children,
in devotion to Rain God Chac Mool,
cast their most precious possessions —
a rubber ball, a gold amulet,
copper bells, a daughter.

Cenote, in the Yucatan evening,
cool and inviting to ZOTZ,
blind, insectivorous God
gifted in echolocation,
to which Man, though blind, came late.
ZOTZ, the bat-like God, swoops,
sips again in mid-flight, tasting,
communing with wide-mouthed *Cenote's*
dark knowledge — the Well of Sacrifice,
a Holy Grail, a chalice
of the feminine arts
of loving give and take.

Venus warns of coming day.
The God of Black Night
slips into the cavern Xibalba —
Underground Heaven.
The waking Sun God projects serpent-like
fingers, wily as the locks of Medusa,
and in a crimson fury emerges

from the crevice hidden by oleander bushes
not far from Old Chichén.

This temple cave—
where the Sun goes at night, rich
in the majesty of alabaster walls,
stalagmites and stalactites
joined in columns—
winds underground.
Here, priests of old performed
the Sacred Mysteries imparted by Kukulkan,
pale-faced and bearded One
the Aztecs called Quetzalcoatl,
Feathered Serpent,
His *Maya* kept alive by the flame
flickering against his Second Coming,
the altar spread with Sacrifice—
meat and fruit—left for priests
after the gods have feasted.

Month 11 — TZEC — June-July

Politics of Religion — The Ball Court — Chichén Itzá — 1961, 1987

Paintings on limestone plaster walls
in ruined temples
show crowds of workers on sloping stands,
opposing teams of players on the court
and priests watching the game
from thatch-roofed platforms.

Carved stone panels suggest the truth:
that these wide-spread games —
were not sport for players
but tragic dramas — the teams
not guilds of workers, schools or colleges,
not Rotarian or Kiwanian societies,
nor handicraft merchants, but Gods —
Sky Gods and Earth Gods — in conflict,
competing for favors, to bring Rain.

Paint crumbles from stuccoed walls,
paintings dim on fig bark pages,
thin evidence for a game of sport,
but murals, chiseled in *bas-relief* on the lower wall
of the Temple of Venus reviewing stand
at Chichén Itzá,
graphically depict the deadly
fascination of the sport,

the fever that accompanies games,
suggest—in lurid tabloid fashion—
that Mayan courts were not for games.
Chisled panels below the temple platform
read like a sports page,
show a game in progress, players arrayed
in shoulder pads and knee pads—
for basketball, an innocent Mayan game?

Their basketball reads more like
a Mercurial game of chess—
priest and shaman using human pawns
on the court—not for sport but for divination—
the winners to be honored—
with Sacrifice.

The object—for players to bounce
rock-hard rubber balls off
their padded shoulders,
elbows, knees and heads,
through a stone or leather ring—
no use of hands permitted—
the game, a scapegoat device
for shaman and priest,
a life-sized horoscope to read
the fates of basketball players,
decided by Gods, earliest of referees.

In the early summer month TZEC,
a crucial season for fertility rites,
the shaman is pressed to decide which
ceremonies to perform
to influence Chac Mool to avert the drought,
to persuade the God of Bees
to pollinate the maize for abundant harvest,
male and female on one stock,

worlds apart.

In summer
when blossoms of *mesquite* beans
wither and fall, when water
in cisterns and surface *aguadas*
drops lower and lower each day,
the chief priest begins to worry twin spectres, Famine
and Epidemic, reported haunting the huts
of workers in the wide-spread
outskirts of their great city-state.

Mayan basketball, a popular sport—
the answer. Hardly a game,
more a gamble, a politics—
human lives manipulated by priest and shaman
obliged by custom to administer rituals,
to read signs and omens.

It is then they call for the game,
the deadly game, to avert disaster.
A few will die for the many—
to point out which god's
grace the priest should evoke,
which evil spirit the shaman must appease.

Who wins the honor of Sacrifice?
The winners? Or, is it the losers
we see decapitated
in the stone-chiseled mural at Chichén Itzá?
We step back
to avoid the splash
of blood . . . .

Month 12 — Xul — July-August

Market Day in Chichicastenango, Guatemala Highlands — 1961

Dour and unfriendly,
faces weathered to leather,
Quiché Maya
walk the mountain trails,
swarm like termites
onto the road to Chichicastenango.

On the market square
they squat among their handicrafts,
scowl at the infrequent *Anglo*
who dares to venture into their villages
hid in the western highlands —
suspicious and fearful,
as if anthropologists
were aliens from Mercury Star of Evening.

These Quiché Indians,
pure stock of ancient Maya,
never truly conquered,
still hide out in remote settlements.
Through summer and winter,
sweltering days and chilling nights,
they wear their white woolen ponchos
of goats' hair, as if woven mantles
were talismans they dare not go without,

charms to protect them
from white-face treachery.

Blazoned on the back of each poncho,
a design—in black—identifies
each wearer's unreachable
village beyond Lake Atitlan—
no road in—isolated
as that perfect hiding place,
the Lunar dark.

Trained from childhood as bearers,
the Quiché trudge like pack animals
through the night,
carry on their backs in wide sisal nets
unbelievable netloads of painted pots
and three-legged stools.
These wares they spread out
on the plaza
for Chi-chi's Sunday marketday,
something to barter
for Jaguar skins and salt.

The men, hostile as savages,
glower at strangers,
glance skeptically at cameras,
tolerate any visitors only
because the local schoolteacher
accompanies them as guide.

A bantam medicine man struts, swings
his smoking wire-handled tin can censer
powerful as a Vatican
gold and jeweled thurible.

As shaman, he decides who are worthy to enter

the little white baroque Spanish church
mildewed on one side
where Highland winds have driven the rains.
He sells them *copal*—balls
of fossil resin and pine needles—
and beeswax candles,
forceful offerings to Saint Thomas.

With odorous puffs from his censer,
he waves them up the staircase,
into the little church,
his power as shaman equal
to that of pope and *brujo*—
the Spanish church, the local healer.

A pilgrim line of *Indios* files out,
weaves a trail like an army of fire ants
across the blood-rich valley,
where fields still smell of the blood
spilled in Alvarado's treachery,
this cleft in the breast
of the Earth Mother, outpost
from which the Quiché
bargained with *Conquistadores*
to accept their Chief,
the very spot where the Spanish slew him.

Across the valley, en route home
to an earlier Time, they pause
at a more primitive altar
to place offerings of *copal*
on the burning hearth
before the smoke-blackened idol
of Rain God Chac Mool.

As they trudge back

to their mountain settlements,
glum of face,
they finger, rosary-like,
their hand-carved amulets of jadeite.

Below, in the valley,
hundreds of living gemstone amulets
turn up their carved primitive faces
every planting season,
this wide, fertile valley
seeded with slaughter
by that strangest of creatures,
half man, half animal,
the horse-man Alvorado,
who, failing to defeat the Quiché in battle,
accept their proviso of peace,
agreed to recognize their chief.

When the *Indios* laid down
their flint points and lances,
sly Alvorado
ordered his horsemen to ride them down,
Spanish soldiers
planting flesh, bone and stone,
seeding the valley
with carved amulets,
worn to show utter distrust
of a white man's face.

Month 13 — YAXKIN — August

The Secret Cave of the Calendar Altar

Don Carlos stops the Jeep
where a stray oleander blooms
among scrub thorn and pine.

> *Señoras*, I know you
> for true *Mayas de otros años,*
> *otras vidas* — other years, other lives.
> Come, let us leave the Jeep, pick
> our way through the underbrush,
> part the branches here
> at the base of the cliff
> and crawl on our bellies
> into this ancient bed
> of an underground stream.
>
> Often as I enter this Sacred Place,
> the skin on my back
> crawls with fear of the Great Unknown,
> as if once known,
> and now only half-remembered.
> You two belong to the Yucatán
> and the Mayab
> as much as I. We will go in . . . .

Breathless, as if entering a cathedral,
we enter an amphibian world

of dank walls and puddled streambed.
My eyes follow the beam
of the electric torch, up, up, up . . . .
It reveals a vaulted ceiling, mineral-streaked
walls columned by tears of the One God.

On a waterfall-polished altar
lies a massive ceremonial stone *metate*
to grind corn for *tortillas* for the Gods,
a pottery urn decorated
with the helical coils of successive lives,
web-entangled mortuary pots filled
with the centuries' congealed darkness.
In this subterraneous Mayan heaven,
priests and medicine men
long renewed the Source
of their Sorceries, of their Sciences.

Not a sound. Nothing moves.
Then, a drip nearby, another farther off.
Slowly Don Carlos moves his torch
down a fluted alabaster wall,
disclosing a Holy of Holies, a great pothole
in the rock of this riverbed,
churned out by millennial gravels
swirling in a whirlpool.

He reveals a low circular stone — an altar,
with eighteen miniature clay idols
outspread around an incised clay disc
with a central, thirsty,
tongue-hanging-out glyph — the Calendar —
each of the idols, a month — surrounded
by twenty jadeite talisman days —
Time a God, all Creation
sacred as our Lady of Guadaloupe today.

The sound of silence,
the bone-penetrating chill,
conjure monk-like phantoms,
whispers of soul-sustaining mantras.
It is as if we were not there . . .
viewing this dream from a far Time.
Winged Time—Sacred Gift to Mankind.
How to catch it, as it flies?

We sense danger, fear of the Unknown—
or is it guilt?
We hurry out, splashing through puddles
on hands and knees.

Who knows what Shadow of Power,
of patronizing arrogance, of greed,
what Evil lurks here?
or what despoilers of Innocence
and Beauty wait outside—or inside
in the labyrinth of passage-ways
lined with shelves—
the empty, bone-filled crypts?

Month 14 — MOL — August and September

Tulum's God of Stored Maize
— Quintana Roo, México — 1962, 1988

Mayan Tulum stands restored
on a cliff above the Caribbean,
on vestiges of archaic walls.
Its ceremonial zone glistens to blindness —
vital impact
born of fossil stone, sun and sea.

Inside a walled compound
white limestone temples
quarried and set in place millennia ago
rise visible again
above a turquoise sea,
that "towering Indian city"
first sighted by the Spanish,
Tulum, a city of Light.

Once priests in Tulum
slept in their hammocks, safe
from civilization's by-products,
vandals, smugglers and *chicleros* — outlaws
who seek the jungle's anonymity.

Slaves, restless on stone floors,
dreamed of living like the high-born ones,
even as descendants of priest,

artisan and slave, surviving in depths
of rain forest will dream, this night.

Tulum — widespread city-state,
powerful complex
of planting and trading rituals —
elaborate ceremonies prescribed
for seeding and harvesting
corn, melons, coconuts,
for coastwise trade in salt and feathers.
Tulum reigned over the east coast of Yucatán
unrivalled for a thousand years
then mysteriously yielded
to the encroaching forest . . . .

Across the centuries, a sea of wild fig
and *sapodilla* trees
washed over temples deserted
by the descending stucco god,
shifted the stones, shrouded
the walled compound in a green fog,
submerged fields into forest.

Cleared after a siesta of a thousand years,
Tulum re-stacks its fragmented stones,
reclaims the walled ceremonial center,
no longer a metropolis extending
suburban arms into Quintana Roo's
chewing gum forest of chicle trees,
but a splendid and ragged outpost
of a truly ingenious culture
that lost faith in its reason for being,
lost sight of the Source of its Light —
how to name it — call it the Sun, KINH,
its sign, the ubiquitous
four-petalled flower blooming unseen.

No exhaustion of soil,
no evidence of warfare or epidemic,
to explain the evacuation . . . .
Tulum, a city deserted before the Spaniards
charged their strange animals
across Lowland Yucatán into Peten
and stumbled on long dead bodies —
the beautiful skeletons of cities,
but found no gold . . . .

Could a growing bureaucracy
of educated rulers and priests
continue to administer
farming, fishing and trading?
continue to feed a growing populace?
to supply city markets
without taxing the laborers and slaves
to exhaustion? Did the workers rise up
and slay the educated elite?

Could it happen again?

Today, a ribbon of paved road
untangles the coastline jungle.
Tourists now flock to Tulum,
like noisy sheep. Let out of cruise ships
anchored in Cancun, they arrive by busses,
or by rented van from Mérida.

But, with Tulum empty at sundown,
KUMKU, the Crocodile-faced God,
wraith-like, walks the walls again.
White faced Luna traces an arc;
stars glimmer like glowworms
on the ceiling of sky above the sea,
Tulum, silent at dusk . . . as before . . . .

But KUMKU, forgotten god of stored maize,
still whispers inside the walls
of a power that was, and is.

In luminescent night, other-worldness
creeps over moist skin.
In this archaic place where there is no Time,
a lost world is still to be found,
another reality experienced,
rich in Hindu MAYA . . . .

Synchronicity? this word MAYA?
found in two worlds, a world apart?

> *If words are winged angels,*
> *intuition must be soul,*
> *ancient wisdoms,*
> *dream-like images, porpoise-like*
> *glimpses of an inner life—*
> *the body, the mind, turned, leaping,*
> *the inside, outside—a vision,*
> *a consciousness of Beauty,*
> *a raw awareness of personhood—*
> *all that separates Mankind*
> *from the animals.*

But should Man ever deny
each animal—each person's god—
a creation of Beauty?
Even the tail-swinging Scorpion,
the dung-eating Beetle, are sacred,
sacred as the Scarab resurrecting,
as the Tarantula spinning MAYA . . . .

> *MAYA, illusory world of the senses,*
> *like sunrays emanating from a center*

to the fertile Serpent
encompassing infinity—
and Mankind dependent on finding
a balancing scale in Nature—
for the fullness of life—
though Terror lurk at one extreme
and the Beauty souls hunger for
at the other—MAYA, ancient field
of dynamic force . . . its resonance
felt . . . in Tulum . . . .

Part IV Introduction to Autumnal Equinox

September-October-November-December
—CHEN-YAX-ZAC-CEH-MAC

Harvest and Moonset

On the sixth day
of the fifteenth month of CHEN,
a cogwheel clicks,
meshes with the universal clock,
and in the slightest hesitation
of a silent shift of gears, summer is gone.
Equinox—a static dynamo—
holds for three days.

On the Great Wheel of Time,
Man and Woman rest from the harvest,
Earth's first fruiting past, her bosom milked dry,
exhausted as the straw and fodder
strewing the fields.

Black thunderheads—benevolent
sky dragons—gather, rumble,
bring brief tropical showers.
Second crop seeds crack.
First leaves unfurl like butterflies
from cocoons into soft equinoctial air.
It is the month of CHEN—Chinese for
LIFE BREAKS OUT OF EARTH.

Harvest Moon, white as daylight,
rises on the eastern horizon.
Field workers fold down
the last husky ears of maize to dry,
to store on the stalk until needed.

Luna X-chel arches her white body
across the arc of sky
toward sunset . . . and moonset.
Shadows cross field and forest,
alien wraiths in white night . . . .

> *They call themselves Maya,*
> *from early priests*
> *reciting legends remembered in dreams*
> *of The Great Valley of Twin Rivers —*
> *a Garden of Asian MAYA — élan vital,*
> *the Tao, a Life Force, a Way —*
> *transported across a quagmire sea*
> *from the East to the West,*
> *long before Phoenicians dared sail*
> *beyond the Gates of Hercules*
> *over the edge of a flat world.*
>
> *Or Africans, like pelicans,*
> *waded a shallower, narrower sea.*
> *The Maya, a people who knew the stars,*
> *could hold a course,*
> *could reach a new world*
> *on balsa rafts, in reed canoes.*
>
> *From wherever they came,*
> *they brought a hierarchy of priests, scribes,*
> *agronomists, astronomers, engineers, masons*
> *experienced in building ziggurats, temples,*
> *pyramids, and alignments of engraved stones,*
> *stelae to stand through centuries*
> *like troops at attention,*
> *feet fixed in Earth, eyes oriented*
> *toward planets and stars.*

After thousands of years,

Time began to run out for the Maya,
the container of Oneness
no longer whole.

Creativity slackened.
Artists worked as engineers,
scribes and poets as merchants.
Toltecs from the north invaded the fringes
of the Mayab, gradually took
control of outlying villages,
organized the workers,
restored Chichén Itzá,
adding ornate facades —
in time all that remained
of Toltecs, absorbed by Mayas, even
as the archaic Olmec were absorbed.

As cities grew, demand increased
for mass-produced pottery and stonework.
Priests vied for material goods.
Farmers left their planting sticks in the fields,
their stone axes in the swamps,
crowded into city centers.

Food and shelter became scarce.
Priests taxed outlying villages, conscripted
soldiers to capture foreign slaves
to work in the fields, the quarries —
with torture the discipline,
as painted in murals at Bonampak.

> *Did an army of young men trained to kill*
> *deplete the corps of talented builders?*
> *remove poetry from the spirit of boys?*
> *hide beauty from the eye? love from the soul?*
> *Did desire for material goods*

obsess and corrupt both ruler and peasant?
Or hunger and disadvantage debauch
a people? bring on thievery and violence?
Did a narrowing of vision
diminish the power of chief priests
and shamans to lead? decrease
their magic MAYA? their meditative vision?
the Light by which they see?

They began to feel the power of possessions,
to withdraw from the community of labor.
Ruler and chief priest surrounded
themselves with luxuries
and a bureaucracy of priests
to train the artisans
in specialized and monotonous occupations.

Early Mayan artists carved and painted
from an aesthetic
more oriental than western.
Like the Asian artist,
the Maya used reality not to convey
an external likeness,
but to express an internal truth,
their affinity for Chinese and Indian art,
another link to their unknown past.

The Maya designed
these magnificent shards with pride
to show the spirit of their time,
the struggles, the doubts
in the souls of a people.

Not to exhort gods of war,
but to perform work as Art,
chant and dance and poetry as prayer

to a Power Intimately Known.
A Power within each creative mind—
works of art to warn a people
to seek to live together on balance
within the order of a personal cosmos
where a Uniqueness of Self,
a Oneness of Space and Time
could be known.

Month 15 — CHEN — October

Tikal's Skyscraper Temple-Tomb
— el Petén, Guatemala — 1967

As Venus Star of Morning
rises in the east,

> *Fly on the blue-green wings*
> *of the scarlet-breasted Quetzal*
> *over the Rain Forest at dawn,*
> *catch sight of Tikal's*
> *skyscraper pyramids,*
> *pink-gold stone towering*
> *above the green Petén,*
> *in pink and gold*
> *crepuscular light.*

> *Let the delicate stone lace*
> *that fell from the roof comb*
> *of Tikal's pyramid-temple-tomb*
> *be restored*
> *and the desecrated stelae*
> *in the plaza below*
> *stand upright again*
> *free of the tropics'*
> *thousand-year embrace . . . .*

> *Let the workers trenching in*
> *under this skyscraper pyramid*

discover the entrance
to the tomb, free the spirit
from the dark,
light the Path,
that Earth's children
may reach the heights
envisioned
by the Power glimpsed within.

As Venus Star of Morning
rises in the east,
young Pietro and his father
hoist wide sisal net packs —
firestarter knots of *ocote* —
onto their backs.

With a cold yam in hand,
they leave their hut of split bamboo,
set out for market.
Tumplines crease their calloused foreheads,
ease the strain of the loads on their backs.
At the paved causeway,
they join a throng of peasant bearers.
Shuffling feet whisper
the *sacbe* — a paved walkway
across lowland swamps drained by canals,
where raised fields produce the maize and beans,
beanvines climbing the cornstalks.

Father and son pass the reed huts of field workers,
enter the walled City of Tikal,
pass shelters of adobe and brick,
where the artisans live
with their women and children —
small cultivated plots,
kitchen gardens of tomatoes and squash.

As they reach the central market plaza
surrounded by stalls and houses
of the new merchant class grown rich
on the labor of peasants and slaves,
they sense confusion.

Woven cotton canopies
shade the hanging merchandise —
skins of Jaguar and Co-ati,
bright feathers of Quetzal,
fresh meats of Tapir and Dog,
weavings, polychrome vases and urns
to decorate homes of merchants,
palaces of priests.

In a shady corner, father and son
spread their firestarter bundles.
The father, uneasy
as on a day of bad omen, wanders off
among the crowds of peasants and slaves,
returns, tells his son trouble is afoot,
to go quickly home, a procession
of priests and guards approaching.
He must not wait for the parade,
but hurry, be a help-mate to his mother.

Mystified, the son watches as peasants
conceal obsidian knives in their sashes,
basalt adzes under their *serapes*
and move apprehensively
toward the acropolis of temples.
He skirts the Great Plaza, glimpses
the Chief Priest descending
the steep and narrow steps of the pyramid
with the aid of slaves.

So this is the day
he had heard his father
and other workers plotting—
the overthrow of the priests,
the taking over of temples and palaces . . . .

With the insight that comes
to the truly distanced,
he wonders
who will lead, who will feed
beautiful, populous Tikal . . .
without the priest administrators?

Haunted by visions of blood
and homeless children,
he races for home
and the arms of his mother,
to wait in their reed hut
on the edge of the tropical forest
for the certain downfall of Tikal,
the fall . . . of a great metropolis . . . .

Month 16 — YAX — October

The Mystery of the Skulls — Copan, Honduras

On the face of the world's time clock
the Mayas' Five New Year Days dimly trace
an ancestral New Year — palimpsest perhaps
of the three-day New Year
of the bearded Chinese priest —
Indios have scant facial hair —
whose portrait statue, *Stele* C, at Copan,
is portrayed with deaths' heads
dangling about his chest.

This bearded Chinese, stands once again,
one of fourteen stone images
of priests wearing headdresses
with feathers, snakes, parrot beaks,
even Indian elephant trunks —
surely chiefs of Asian origin.

Monumental ceremonial works uncovered,
the jungle pushed back; carvings, cleaned
of jungle roots and restored, stand upright,
reveal stonework intricate as filigree.

Copan, city of *stelae,* and the unique
Hieroglyphic Staircase — sixty-three stone steps —
not for climbing, but a work of art,
carved with over two thousand blocks

of unread glyphs—handsome
and stylized arcane Mayan writing—
on the rises, and on the banisters,
serpentine fertility motifs.

These jewels of Mayan art
weather once again in place
in the Ceremonial Court,
an intimate amphitheatre bounded
by low stairs on four sides, seats
for a city of fifty thousand,
monuments to the greatness, the Oneness
of the Will to Create,
the Time-less-ness of Now.

Past, Present, Future, All One in Copan,
a prosperous city-state for 500 years,
the last *stele* consecrated
with a date of bars and dots
equivalent to 800 A.D.

In prosperous Copan Valley, cultivated Earth
excites a vortex of energy.
Rich alluvial soils
produce great gold tobacco leaves
and food in abundance.
The River Copan flows gently by,
below the desecrated, deserted acropolis.
Today, light breezes, disembodied spirits,
waft through arches of broken temples.

Across the Mayab it is said
that workers came to believe
in *Metnal*—a dark afterlife
of cold, hunger and weariness.
The evidence abounds in Copan.

A stairway incised
with balustrades of human heads
leads to the reviewing stand.
Here artists carved skulls as decoration —
a prescience of disaster,
manifest by stone carvers.

Greed and cruelty appeared
in grotesque faces
of the later human sculptures —
an ambiance of death in the carved
stone skulls of Copan. But why?
No evidence of war, epidemic,
starvation or climate change.

Astronomers charting the turning
of planets, left their look-out posts.
Priests abandoned the acropolis of temples
as if threatened by invasion, or plague.
Did they gather a council, call for a ballgame
to augur the will of their Three-in-One?
Did they agree to go? But where?

Or did workers and foreign slaves
rise up against an oppressive elite,
force them to flee? the uneducated try in vain
to operate a complex economy?

Copan, in the ninth century,
a truly advanced culture,
practiced the arts and sciences:
agriculture on a large scale, herbal medicine,
engineering design, hydraulics,
monumental construction, sculpture,
inventions of paper, cement and plaster,
the calendar, music on marimba, flute,

and drum, art in glyphic writing, carving,
painting, dentistry with inlaid jade,
astronomy, mathematics.

Then, suddenly, or gradually, Copan
is deserted, a culture suffocated
under encroaching wilderness,
temple foundations twisted,
the Mother-Father God denied,
the power of the phallus
unmet by tenderness,
a city devoured by jungle hungers,
crying to be rediscovered,
its early monuments interpreted,
its elegant glyphic writing more fully translated —
in a more enlightened age —
an age still to come.

Month 17 — ZAC — October-November

Prophecy — The Catacombs of Kaminaljuyú, Guatemala — 1961

Fog and drizzle envelop
the mountain road,
shroud the archaic earthen pyramid.

Kaminaljuyú is Ninevah,
excavated capital of First Earth,
its antediluvian beginnings
hidden in Mankind's earliest myths.

A witness, basaltic lava
reveals how the restless gods of Earth
shrugged, spewed ash, wildfire and magma,
sucked up the seas in their thirst,
toppled Second Earth.

Only a shed of corrugated iron
protects the diggings
attended by an aged, monk-like Maya
undismayed by mist and rain.

> *To Mayas,*
> *All Time is One Whole —*
> *Past, Present, Future, All One,*
> *All Now, One Continuum.*

Typifying Wise Old Man, the Mayan guard
receives the occasional visitor,
gracious as a priest welcoming pilgrims
come to reverence a legend —
the legend of the three lost worlds:

> *The First, by Flood.*
> *The Second, by Quake —*
> *and Upheaval of Earth.*
> *The Third, by World Sweeping*
> *Solar Wind. The Next, Mayan*
> *soothsayers portend, by Fire.*

> *Fire storms that flash with Light*
> *equal to Sun . . . .*
> *Lightning that flashes in a fanning cloud.*
> *Fire that girdles the world,*
> *exhausts the air . . . .*

> *Daimonic energy released from matter . . .*
> *guiding spirits . . . disembodied . . .*
> *the Fourth Earth, cooling . . . .*

Man's ultimate fate —
to eat of the fruit of the Tree
of the Knowledge of Good and Evil?
and Adam, too immature to handle it?

The guard of this archaic temple —
this pyramid of lava mud
weathering in the gray drizzle
that marries Earth and Sky —
the Ancient One shuffles over
the worn earthen floor
to light a ceramic handlamp —
a portrait head

of curly bearded Quetzalcoatl.
Flames leap like Truth
from his three beard curls.

The old Maya
lives his role as priest
with dignity. With caution,
he leads us down to the crypt
below the lava pyramid,
descends mouldering steps —
slippery and worn —
descends to archaic Mayan catacombs.

Smoky light from resinous fire
of *ocote* pine knots
flickers from a round altar of basalt.
A labyrinth of tunnels fans out
like petals on a sunflower,
curving galleries, catacombs
with shallow shelves
where skulls stare,
where priests and ancestors of priests
lie ravished by the ages, still grasping
ceremonial knives of obsidian
in bony-fingered hands, as if to stave off
rot of flesh, decay of culture.

A culture rooted in Asia —
in Ninevah, or Ur.

Month 18 — CEH — November-December

A Voice Rises from Inside the Tomb
— Palenque — 1967

*Visitors to the truly splendid Museo Archeologico
in Mexico City can see the sarcophagus and
the artifacts removed from the Palenque pyramid
reassembled in a replica of the tomb —
could, until stolen in 1989.*

The Maya themselves,
after a thousand — two thousand —
years, have no bodily memory
of funereal drum beat,
of priests in opulent regalia —
Quetzal feathers, animal masks —
marching in procession
to hide the body
and confine the spirit of a chief
inside a pyramid tomb.
Quiet as if vowed to silence,
they encouraged a belief
accepted by archeologists —
American pyramids contain no tombs,
a popular myth, dispelled in 1952.

Mexican archeologist Alberto Ruz —
a seer with channel vision into Mayan mind —
hacked his way with *machete,*

through thick poles of bamboo,
screen-like branches of *cedrela,*
towering mahogany, silk-cotton *sapote* trees,
the rain forest tangle of vines,
to the pyramid known to nearby villagers
as Palenque, its ceremonial center
hidden in jungle growth
ruthless and destructive as Man himself.

He climbed the up-turned, tall steps
through roots thick and strong
as boa constrictors.
Like a mountain climber,
he secured each foothold,
mounted broken steps
to the top—flat as a giant *ceiba*
timbered in virgin forestland.

Behind a a colonnaded porch
he found the inner sanctum of a temple
with two walls of stone-carved
hieroglyphic writing.
He named it
Temple of the Inscriptions.

> *How many fingers have traced and retraced*
> *this deep-cut, beautiful, cursive writing?*
> *—with its power to evoke sorrow and regret,*
> *as military monuments do,*
> *even for men we did not know.*

As he measured the fitted stone floor
under centuries of dust and debris,
Ruz uncovered a flagstone
with a double row of round holes—
a removable capstone to a stairway

descending to the underworld.

For two years, Ruz and crew
scratched like armadillos,
excavated rubble from a stairs,
where, at ground level,
they discovered
a tomb sealed with a fitted stone slab,
and behind it, a magnificent sarcophagus.

Partial translation
of the temple's inscription
revealed the burial date—692 A.D.—
and the name of the ruler buried below—
Pacal—forgotten
for twelve hundred and sixty years . . . .

For those who climb the pyramid to listen,
ear to the capstone,
his still incarcerated spirit,
at home here, repeats his story . . . .

> I, Pacal, feel the throbbing beat
> of raindrops
> falling through layers of years,
> like the layers of leaves
> of the jungle canopy
> concealing my Palenque.
>
> Sinuous roots twist the stones.
> Trees grow from pyramidal platforms
> in the rain forest, as they
> conceal my three gem-like temples—
> Sun, Cross, Foliated Cross—
> on whose panels my artisans sculptured
> names and dates in intricate low relief.

Roots like giant serpents
creep into aqueducts,
invade empty corridors, choke
the four-story throat of my palace,
rubble the outside stairs
to the Temple of the Inscriptions
above my hiding place,
a forgotten tomb inside a sleeping pyramid—
in this lost city of Palenque
blanketed by rain forest.

I dream . . . my skull, whitened
by the centuries' airless polishing,
lies here undisturbed
under a mosaic mask of jade,
my eyes jet black obsidian,
my crown jade, my earplugs
inlaid with jade and mother of pearl.

The bones of my arms and chest
lie collapsed under bracelets of jade beads,
necklaces of jade carved
in the shapes of flowers and fruit,
a breastplate of tubular jade beads.
Rings fall from my bony fingers.
Neither the jade Sun God, nor the stone axes,
nor the bones of youths sacrificed
outside my burial chamber
can serve me now . . . .

Each year in the month of MOL,
all nature ripening toward harvest,
artists and artisans carve and mold
new idols of jade and of clay.
Priests and novitiates

paint new altar utensils
green and blue, colors sacred
to nourishing Earth, nurturing Sky.

Slaves—foreign captives
who ventured too near our city—
haul great slabs of stone
from near-by sierra in rope slings
on their collective shoulders.

Sculptor-priests and artists
with sharpened flints
carve glyphs into clay, stucco and stone,
on wall panels and temple inscriptions
to record the names and years
of a dynasty of rulers—my family.

Each fifty-two years, to please
our many Gods-in-One, we level
older temples, fill foundations,
consecrate ourselves, rebuild anew . . . .

But after my sons—and their sons' sons—
our people disappeared
from the ceremonial plaza . . . .
Did I hear the clash
of soldiers' shields and spears?
Did my rotting flesh
feel the flash of obsidian darts
before my people fled?

Chiapas' dusky rain forest
overran deserted Palenque.
Temple roof-combs of stone lace
fell to Earth.
Ceiba trees clutched a once-great city

to the bosom of the forest.

Few there are to climb
the broken staircase
to the Temple of Inscriptions,
none to read the carved stones telling
of the centuries of reigns of my family,
of the great architectural works attempted,
accomplished by my people.

May the One — our Mother-Father God —
the Trinity of Sun, Rain and Earth —
speak now to the man I hear
measuring the floor
of the temple over my head,
show him the movable capstone seal,
my rubble-filled stairs,
and may he decipher
the carved inscription on the wall,
call my name, Pacal.

Pacal, suspended in Time,
down shifts between the centuries.
Neither his Time, nor that
of this impoverished Third Mayan World —
the land, the power
still in the hands of the few —
can serve the many.
By the hundreds, the thousands,
Mayas abandon the land,
crowd into electrified villages and towns,
retain little of their heritage,
or does it sleep, waiting for
a more auspicious time to be recalled?

May the Light within dark tombs,

nourish the spirit, nurture the wish to know.

May this fluorescence
flourish like white mushrooms
in dank caves,
this luminescence shining unperceived
empower Mankind
to grow in mind and spirit
from fertile spoors left on the Path
by Mentors and Leaders of the past,
risking, accepting change,
extending their reach to newer worlds,
newer tasks thought impossible,
undreamed of,
one thousand years, one year, ago.

Epilogue

The Eternal Song
—Answer to the Dry Season

Astronomer, mathematician,
chronologist, agronomist,
creative Mayan scientists
uncovered truths
relevant for an economy
dependent on a partnership
between Nature and Man.

The Maya saw it clearly
for over two thousand years:
theirs, a fertility cult,
a culture dependent on maize
and on workers to cultivate great fields.

Phalli transfigured their art
and architecture—upright stones,
as at Cobá,
and on the wall near the ball court
at Chichén Itzá,
reminders of spiraling Life,
ejaculation
the projection into Eternity, a Sacrament.

The double helix,
moulded on their pottery,
intertwines, repeats its intricate designs,
as the essence of life, the DNA, revolves
like a spiral staircase,
drawing its strength, its magnetism,
from a Centerpoint,

as Earth draws upon the invisible dynamics
of its Source.

Copulating Jaguars subtly enhance
the handles of ritual vessels
from the Ulúa Valley in Honduras,
cylindrical jars
of design and proportion so radiant, so pure,
of clay so white, they appear
translucent.
Finger-carved in continuous coils of glyphs,
curved squares, divinely and purely beautiful
as white alabaster, they gather Light —
could Mankind but read the Word.

Fertility symbols bless matrimonial hammocks,
and wall hangings woven of henequen and hemp —
and nylon — brighten displays in village markets
and artists' *bodegas* today.

Guardians of Ancient Wisdoms, the Maya
employed mathematics in their cosmology,
created a sign for completion,
after a count of twenty, the Principle of ZERO.
a cipher that transports back in Time,
forward into Space, and deep, within.

> *Ancient Maya — from wherever they came —*
> *or, born in this lush, swampy Eden —*
> *created a truly phenomenal civilization*
> *based on their oriental concept*
> *of being in and of the natural world —*
> *they, themselves, a part*
> *of the animal kingdom —*
> *in and of Space and Time — one Whole —*
> *with vestiges of Light*

absorbed in the body of a people
in passage through the millennia,
through Egypt and Arabia,
The Fertile Crescent, Mesopotamia,
India, China, and the Islands . . . .

The horns of the crescent
inform a circle. The circle squares—
creates a talisman of great beauty, like
the flaked obsidian edge, the glass wall,
where today's physicists and mystics reach
to touch, to balance, to clasp hands, to stand.

A civilization—akin only to the Chinese—
obliterated, lost to historical account.

Within one hundred years,
building ceased in city sites
throughout the Yucatán Mayab—from west of Palenque
to east of Copan. Who knows why?

Scientists, philosophers, too,
the Maya understood the material body
is not Reality, is only a convenience
for a few score years.

Mayan priests, like the Chinese
with I Ching,
grasped the Essence of Joy,
of Sorrow, of Gratitude,
understood the Elixir of Life.

Early Maya felt the élan vital
coursing their veins, followed—
or led—the Ancient Chinese Tao—
the Way, the Path. They knew

the Motherhood of God—Earth Mother,
Sun, Rain, Soil—the Three-in-One Source.

All planets, galaxies, seen and unseen—
One Undivided Whole. Inner and Outer Lives,
One, magnetized. One World, Time and Space—
This Time, This Body, sacred. The Earth
and her Creatures, One Inter-dependent Whole.

While vandal hordes ransacked Europe
for thousands of years,
the Maya in Middle America—
like the Egyptians, Mesopotamians, Chinese,
Greeks, Romans and Arabs, in turn—
guarded the Treasury of Mankind's
discovery, invention and insight—
the archetypal memory, passed in the genes.

What voice, what music,
filled the Mayan heart
with Wisdom Songs of the Ages?
Was it Yahweh? or some earlier vision
of Light? avatar of Creative Spirit?

The Christ? Buddha? Quetzalcoatl?
Kukulkan? Or an inherent curiosity
to know Truth? to be—to be unique?
to be aware? to be free—to know,
to seek to know?

The music of the Mayan calendar
floats like a trailing veil of haze
on the evening air of the Peninsula.
Mayan shadows haunt restored temples
and mounds of overgrown rubble
deep in the rain forests of the Mayab.

In swaying and abrading vines,
ghostly Mayan voices
murmur and sigh at twilight.

> *From where did they come?*
> *And why did they disappear?*
> *And who was Quetzalcoatl?*
> *The old mysteries — mysteries still.*

Postscript

Reflections
— To End is to Make a Beginning

Had they come farther
on the Path than we have come?
Have we slipped more easily and
more deeply into Materialism than they?
Do we mis-use, abuse our Mother Earth any less
than they who slashed the Forest, burned the Trees?
Did the affluence of chief and priest, the educated elite,
become unbearable, to the laborers, to the foreign slaves?

Mayan priests and priestesses believed in Cycles, counted
in repeating units: 20 days, 18 months, 360 days; 52 years;
7200 days, 20 years — a katun; 144,000 days, 400 years —
a baktun. They saw the Order, the Mystery, the
depths of Mathematics, perceived an Orderly
Universe whose greatest Mysteries are
Space and Time, part of a greater
Whole to be found on the Path.

5 March 1990

About the Author

Mary Belle "Peg" Campbell, free-lance journalist from age 15, teacher and counselor while her two children were growing up, initiated The American Field Service foreign scholarship program in her community, Rocky River, a suburb of Cleveland, Ohio. To support her interests in international friendship, she turned to a business career and to travel writing.

In 1973, she retired with husband Walter J. Campbell to Whispering Pines, NC, "in search of a more creative life." She found it in a series of Creative Writing classes and workshops across the country and at the Ezra Pound retreat Schloss Brunnenburg in Italy, where she studied for a month with poets Ronald H. Bayes and Princess Mary de Rachewiltz. She began to publish poetry in 1976 in the little literary magazines, university reviews and North Carolina anthologies. Her first collection, *The Business of Being Alive*, was published by St. Andrews Press in 1982. "Peg" is now an instructor of Creative Writing at Sandhills Community College, Pinehurst, NC.

In late 1987 she founded Scots Plaid Press and Persephone Press as an adjunct to St. Andrews Press to design and publish aesthetic paperback books of poetry, with emphasis on the beauty of carefully selected type fonts, quality papers, and artistic illustration. Some limited editions are hand-sewn with deckle edge papers.

This first edition of *Light from Dark Tombs*
was designed and composed at
Briarpatch Press in Davidson, North Carolina.
The typeface is Zapf Elliptical.

The Mayan glyphs for the 18 months and the five fateful days called *Uayeb* are taken from J. Eric S. Thompson's *Mayan Hieroglyphs Without Tears* (London: The British Museum, 1971).

Book List 1991
Persephone Press Poetry Series
Adjunct to St. Andrews Press

1 Nina Wicker, **Winter and Wild Roses, Seven Haiku** - 24p $4.95
   "sensitive . . . an economy of words and phrases" — Chas. B.
   Dickson   Hand-sewn   Now in second edition

2 Mary Carleton Snotherly, **Stars to Steer By — A Galaxy of Poems**   7.95
   - 32p "Drawings by Cissy Russell add to the magic of the
   words." — Sam Ragan   "New ways to perceive the world, to
   remember the magic." — Margaret Baddour   Hand-sewn
   Deckle edges

3 Gladys Hughes, **A CELL — A DOOR — Selected Poems** - 48p   8.95
   "A beautiful book . . . poems of great strength." — Sam Ragan
   1989 Award-winning Book — Poetry Council of North Carolina
   Cover art by Thomas Cox Edgerton

4 Mary Belle Campbell, **Light from Dark Tombs** - 104p   9.95
   A Traveler's Map to Mysteries of the Ancient Maya   "The
   poet strives to bring what is dark into 'white clarity,' that state
   of illumination toward which the world moves in Mayan sacred
   text." — Kathryn Stripling Byer   "Good news . . . the world
   needs it." — William Stafford

5 Tom Smith, **The Broken Iris — Fifty Haiku** - 32p   7.95
   "These haiku cut across cultural boundaries . . . express the
   oneness of us all, confronted by nature." — Dr. Joyce Thomas

6 Sallie Nixon, **Spiraling — Selected Poems** - 32p   7.95
   "full of light, and I feel I am standing in it." — Mark Van Doren
   "A fresh strangeness . . ." — Richard Eberhardt
   "a writer at the peak of her gifts" — Shelby Stephenson
   Deckle edges   Calligraphy

7 Carolyne Kyles, **Lines to Someone — Selected Poems** - 32p   7.95
   "a palpable grasp of life's inaccessibles . . . meticulous in her
   craft . . . poetry worthy of the name." — Sallie Nixon
   Art by Andrea Boggs   Calligraphy by Gladys Horne   Deckle edge

8 Joe Chace, **The Red Ghost, Poems of Place** - 32 p   7.95

To order, add $1.50 per book for postage and handling. Mail check to:

St. Andrews Press
St. Andrews College
Laurinburg, NC 28352

or

Persephone Press
Aesthetic Chapbooks
22-B Pine Lake Drive
Whispering Pines, NC 28327-9388
Tel. 919/949-3993